ANCIENT AND MEDIEVAL PEOPLE

The Japanese Samurai

Louise Park
and Timothy Love

Marshall Cavendish
Benchmark

New York

This edition first published in 2010 in the United States of America by Marshall Cavendish Benchmark.

Marshall Cavendish Benchmark
99 White Plains Road
Tarrytown, NY 10591
www.marshallcavendish.us

All Internet sites were available and accurate when sent to press.

First published in 2009 by
MACMILLAN EDUCATION AUSTRALIA PTY LTD
15–19 Claremont Street, South Yarra 3141

Visit our website at www.macmillan.com.au or go directly to www.macmillanlibrary.com.au

Associated companies and representatives throughout the world.

Library of Congress Cataloging-in-Publication Data

Park, Louise, 1961–
    The Japanese samurai / by Louise Park and Timothy Love.
        p. cm. – (Ancient and medieval people)
    Includes index.
    ISBN 978-0-7614-4448-0
    1. Samurai–Juvenile literature. 2. Military art and science–Japan–Juvenile literature. 3. Japan–History, Military–Juvenile literature. I. Love, Timothy. II. Title.
    DS827.S3P375 2010
    355.00952–dc22
                        2009003573

Edited by Julia Carlomagno
Text and cover design by Cristina Neri, Canary Graphic Design
Page layout by Cristina Neri, Canary Graphic Design
Photo research by Legend Images
Illustrations by Colby Heppéll, Giovanni Caselli, and Paul Konye

Printed in the United States

Acknowledgments
The author and the publisher are grateful to the following for permission to reproduce copyright material:

Front cover photo: Matsumoto Castle, Japan © Alan Crawford/iStockphoto; parchment © Selahattin BAYRAM/iStockphoto

Photos courtesy of: Background photos throughout: old paper © peter zelei/iStockphoto; mosaic tiles © Hedda Gjerpen/iStockphoto; bamboo © Florea Marius Catalin/iStockphoto; gate and tree © Brandon Laufenberg/iStockphoto;fighting samurai figures © Andrej Godjevac/iStockphoto; riding samurai figure © Imre Cikajlo/iStockphoto; © Kristof Degreef/Dreamstime.com, **24**; Art by Sid Ka'imi Campbell, www.warriorartworks.com/, **29**; DEA/A. DAGLI ORTI/Getty Images, **23**; Japanese School/Getty Images, **14**; Sean Sexton/Getty Images, **25**; Mansell/Time Life Pictures/Getty Images, **11**; Giovanni Caselli's Universal Library Unlimited, **6, 9, 12, 13, 15, 16, 17, 18, 19, 20, 22, 27, 30**; © Alan Crawford/iStockphoto, **4** (castle); Photolibrary/Mary Evans Picture Library, **8**; Wikimedia Commons, **10, 21, 28**.

Sources for quotes used in text: Bushido code translations from Random House's/Japanese-English, English-Japanese Dictionary, **24**; Translation for poem by Shibata Katsuie from Wikipedia, **29**.

The authors and publisher wish to advise that to the best of their ability they have tried to verify dates, facts, and the spelling of personal names and terminology. The accuracy and reliability of some information on ancient civilizations is difficult in instances where detailed records were not kept or did not survive.

1 3 5 6 4 2

Contents

Glossary Words

When a word is printed in **bold**, you can look up its meaning in the Glossary on page 31.

Who Were the Japanese Samurai?

The Japanese samurai were soldiers who served the **aristocracy** in Japan. They were **elite** professional warriors who were well-trained, **armored**, and heavily armed.

Feudal Japan

Feudal Japan was a **monarchy** run by the **emperor**. It had four different periods.

❖ The Kamakura period (1183–1335 CE) was named for the town of Kamakura, where the empire was based.

❖ The Muromachi period (1336–1576) was named for the Muromachi area in the city of Kyoto.

❖ The Sengoku period (1578–1600) was a period of civil war between samurai **clans** and **daimyo**.

❖ The Edo period (1603–1868) was named for the capital city of Edo, which today is known as Tokyo.

WHAT'S IN A NAME?

Samurai

The name *samurai* was given to those who served in the military **nobility**. It means "to serve."

Japanese Samurai Timeline

1180
The first shogun, Minamoto no Yoritomo, defeats the Taira clan during the Gempei War

1336–1573
The Muromachi period

1185–1336
The Kamakura period

| 1100 | 1200 | 1300 | 1400 | 150 |

4

Key
Where Japanese samurai were found
Scale
100 miles
150 kilometers

Sea of Japan

JAPAN

SOUTH KOREA

•Okehazama
Kyoto •

PACIFIC OCEAN

Japanese samurai lived and fought in the group of islands known as Japan.

Quick Facts

Who Ruled the Japanese Samurai?
The Japanese samurai were ruled by the emperor and by a shogun.

❖ The emperor was the ruler of Japan. During Japan's feudal period, the emperor became a **figurehead**.

❖ The shogun was a Japanese military general who led the most powerful samurai clan. A shogun also held political power, and his clan became known as the shogunate.

The Formation of the Japanese Samurai

The Japanese samurai formed during the Heian period, which came before the feudal period. Between 794 and 1185, the Japanese government established an army of mounted horsemen by **recruiting** professional soldiers. These soldiers were members of the Japanese nobility and they were loyal to the emperor. During the Heian period, shogunates began to take control of Japan. Each shogunate was led by a powerful shogun, or military general. Shoguns developed private samurai armies to **conquer** and protect land. Before long, professional soldiers found their way into these private armies and became samurai.

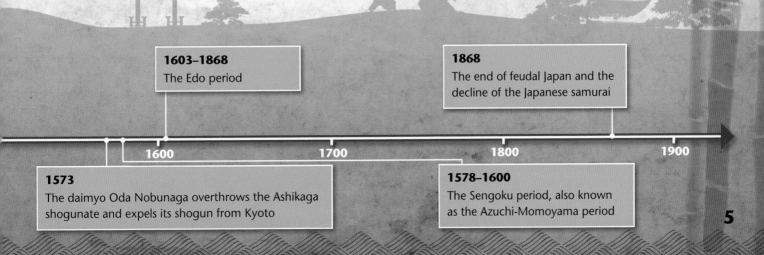

1603–1868
The Edo period

1868
The end of feudal Japan and the decline of the Japanese samurai

1600   1700   1800   1900

1573
The daimyo Oda Nobunaga overthrows the Ashikaga shogunate and expels its shogun from Kyoto

1578–1600
The Sengoku period, also known as the Azuchi-Momoyama period

5

The Japanese Feudal System

Between the 1100s and 1800s, Japan was run according to a feudal system, which is a social system with a strong **hierarchy**. Under the feudal system, the samurai and shoguns held large amounts of power.

The Rise of the Samurai

The period just before the beginning of feudal Japan was known as the Heian period, and it gave rise to two powerful samurai clans. These clans were the Minamoto, or Genji, and the Taira, or Heike. Conflicts between these two clans turned into **civil wars**. Eventually the Minamoto clan gained control of Japan. Their leader, Minamoto no Yoritomo, established Japan's first shogunate and became the first shogun. Throughout the feudal period, these clans continued to fight for land and power.

Samurai rode on horseback and fought on behalf of a clan.

The Social Classes of Feudal Japan

Japan had eight social classes. The nobility made up around 10 percent of Japan's population, and included the emperor, the shogun, daimyo, samurai, and ronin. The other 90 percent of the population were peasants, artisans, and merchants.

Under Japan's feudal system, most people were from the lower social classes.

THE EMPEROR
Japan's **monarch** and head of the **imperial family**. He was a figurehead who was generally under the shogun's power.

THE SHOGUN
Japan's military leader and head of the samurai army. He also held political power, and his political office was the shogunate.

DAIMYO
Members of the warrior class who ran the shogun's lands and estates. They were the highest rank of samurai nobility.

SAMURAI
Professional warriors who were loyal to the shogun and daimyo.

RONIN
Paid professional soldiers who fought during wars. They were a lower class of samurai who did not pledge loyalty to daimyo or the shogun.

ARTISANS, MERCHANTS, AND PEASANTS
Artisans made equipment, tools, and weapons, and merchants sold goods and produce. Peasants were farmers and fishers who gave most of their produce to daimyo and the shogun in exchange for the right to live on the land.

Shogunates of the Feudal Period

The Kamakura shogunate, the Ashikaga shogunate, and the Tokugawa shogunate each controlled feudal Japan during a different period. These shogunates aimed to conquer large amounts of land in order to **consolidate** their power.

The Kamakura Shogunate

The Kamakura shogunate ruled Japan during the Kamakura period. It was established by Minamoto no Yoritomo in 1192, when he seized power during the Gempei War by defeating the Taira clan. During the Kamakura shogunate, a system of **inheritance** was established so that the title of shogun could be passed down through the family line. Daimyo were placed in charge of **provinces** and samurai began to report to the daimyo. The last family to rule this shogunate was the Hojo family. The Kamakura shogunate ended when the Hojo family was overthrown in 1336.

Minamoto no Yoritomo was the first shogun of Japan and all daimyo reported to him.

The Ashikaga Shogunate

The Ashikaga shogunate ruled Japan during the Muromachi period. It was established by Ashikaga Takauji in 1336, when he sided with the emperor against the Kamakura shogun. However, the emperor took on extra duties following the fall of the Kamakura shogunate, which meant that Ashikaga had less power than the previous shogun. As a result, the Ashikaga shogunate was weaker than the Kamakura shogunate and had to rely heavily on the loyalty of its daimyo and samurai. The daimyo began fighting one another for power and, eventually, civil war broke out. The Ashikaga shogunate collapsed when the daimyo Oda Nobunaga drove the Ashikaga shogun out of Kyoto in 1573.

The Tokugawa shogunate is named after Tokugawa Ieyasu, who seized power following the Battle of Sekigahara.

The Tokugawa Shogunate

The Tokugawa shogunate ruled Japan during the Edo period. It was established after the Battle of Sekigahara in 1600 and became the longest-lasting shogunate of the feudal period. When Tokugawa Ieyasu became shogun, he established a strict class hierarchy in which the shogun and his samurai held power over the peasants. In 1869, this shogunate was overthrown and the fifteenth Tokugawa shogun **resigned**. This marked the end of the feudal period.

IN PROFILE: Minamoto no Yoritomo

In Profile

NAME: Minamoto no Yoritomo
ALSO KNOWN AS: The first shogun
BORN: 1147
DIED: 1199

Minamoto no Yoritomo was born into the Minamoto clan and went on to become the first shogun of Japan. While he only ruled for seven years, the system of shogunates he founded lasted until 1868.

In 1158, Minamoto no Yoritomo was given his first court title, or recognition, by the emperor. It was awarded to him because he was related to the imperial family. However, in 1159 civil war broke out and many members of the Minamoto clan were executed. Minamoto no Yoritomo was exiled and did not return for nearly twenty years.

Notable Moment

In 1185, Minamoto no Yoritomo defeated the Taira clan during the Gempei War. This was a major victory for the Minamoto clan. Following this battle, Minamoto no Yoritomo seized control of Japan and established the Kamakura shogunate.

Minamoto no Yoritomo Timeline

1130   1140   1150   1160

1147
Born into the Minamoto clan

1158
Earns his first court title and is appointed administrator

Creating the Shogunate System

Minamoto no Yoritomo created the shogunate system, in which power was handed down through a family. Under this new system, daimyo upheld law and order in the provinces and samurai conquered land on behalf of the shogun. Upon his death, Yoritomo was **succeeded** by his eldest son, Minamoto no Yoriie, who became the second Kamakura shogun.

What You Should Know About...

Minamoto no Yoritomo

❖ Yoritomo was exiled in his youth after joining his father at a rebellion against the Taira clan. His father died at this rebellion.

❖ Yoritomo's eldest son Yoriie was assassinated after he became shogun. Yoritomo's second son, Sanetomo, then became the third Kamakura shogun.

Minamoto no Yoritomo became Japan's first shogun at a large ceremony in 1192.

1170   1180   1190   1200

1180
Joins a rebellion against the Taira clan and is defeated

1185
Defeats the Taira clan and wins the Gempei War

1192
Establishes the Kamakura shogunate and becomes the first shogun

Samurai Armor

Samurai armor developed over hundreds of years as battle strategies changed and new technologies developed. However, the **components** of samurai armor remained the same.

Components of Samurai Armor

Samurai armor was made up of several components, including:

❖ a helmet, or *kabuto*

❖ a neck guard, or *shikoro*

❖ a torso plate, or *cuirass*

❖ shoulder guards, or *dō*

❖ sleeve armor, or *kote*

❖ an armored apron that protected the thighs, or *haidate*

❖ shin guards, or *suneate*

These components were made from several metal plates, which were laced together with leather cord. Lacing armor together was a special art and craftsmen often used certain colors and patterns to indicate which clan a samurai belonged to. Tight, elaborate lacing was used for high-ranking samurai while wider lacing was used for those in lower ranks. The plates were then coated with lacquer, or protective coating, to prevent them from rusting. Finally, they were tied together horizontally with a silk cord called *kebiki odoshi*.

Samurai wore armor to protect their bodies during battle.

Oyoroi Armor

Oyoroi armor had a boxlike appearance and was worn by mounted samurai. During the 1300s, battles began to be fought on foot, rather than on horses. Over time, oyoroi armor was replaced with other types of armor because it was so heavy and difficult to move around in. An oyoroi suit of armor could weigh up to 62 pounds(28 kilograms) and it lacked the flexibility needed for hand-to-hand combat.

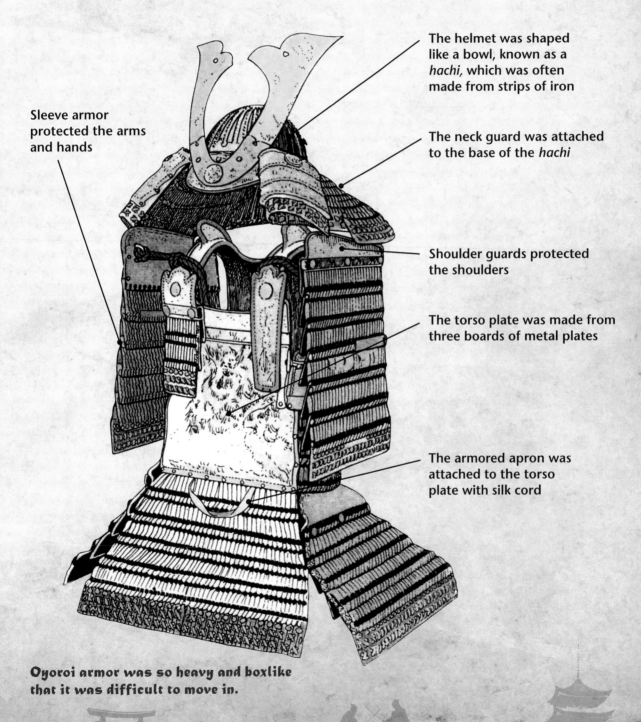

Sleeve armor protected the arms and hands

The helmet was shaped like a bowl, known as a *hachi,* which was often made from strips of iron

The neck guard was attached to the base of the *hachi*

Shoulder guards protected the shoulders

The torso plate was made from three boards of metal plates

The armored apron was attached to the torso plate with silk cord

Oyoroi armor was so heavy and boxlike that it was difficult to move in.

Do Maru Armor

Do maru armor wrapped around the body, and it was lighter and more flexible than oyoroi armor. It is believed that do maru armor existed before oyoroi armor but was only worn by ronin. When hand-to-hand combat began to take place, this type of armor was also adopted by the samurai. It was worn well into the 1500s and was often made from a combination of leather and metal.

Do maru armor allowed samurai to move around more freely than oyoroi armor.

The neck guard was curved to allow the head and neck extra movement

The torso plate wrapped around the body and tied at the side

Leather plates protected the arms and legs, allowing for extra movement

Shin guards protected the shins

Haramaki Armor

Haramaki armor wrapped around the body in a similar way to do maru armor, but it tied at the back rather than the side. It was used until the Edo period in the mid–1800s, although it never became the main form of samurai armor.

WHAT'S IN A NAME?
Do Maru and Haramaki

The term *do maru* means "body wrap." Some say that the word *haramaki* means "belly warmer."

An eye guard known as a *fukigaeshi* rolled up to give a samurai full vision

Leather plates protected the arms, allowing for extra movement

The torso plate tied at the back. It was often reinforced with a plate that extended from the back of the neck to the hip.

Shin guards protected the shins

Haramaki armor was similar to do maru armor, but the torso plate tied at the back.

Samurai Weapons

The samurai used many different weapons over the centuries. The most **enduring** weapons were the bow and arrow, the sword, and the pole.

The Bow and Arrow

The bow and arrow was the weapon of choice for samurai warriors for centuries. Training with the bow and arrow on horseback was considered a noble art and it was restricted to high-ranking samurai. Samurai were skilled horsemen who rode using only their legs when shooting arrows from their bows. As he fired an arrow, a samurai could not sway in the saddle or he would fall from the running horse.

During the Heian period, samurai often practiced their archery skills in competitions.

Quick Facts

How Important Was Archery During the Heian Period?

Archery grew in importance during the Heian period as samurai were trained and archers were celebrated.

❖ Each samurai clan had archery ranges to train their archers. Training techniques were developed and competitions were held.

❖ Minamoto no Tametomo was a famous archer during this period. He is believed to have sunk a ship with a single arrow. Legend says that Tametomo's left arm was 6 inches (15 centimeters) longer than his right, which allowed him to release powerful shots.

Samurai often carried bows
and arrows into battle.

The Longbow

The longbow, or *daikyu*, was preferred by most samurai because it
could shoot metal arrows across long distances. A longbow was often
more than 6.6 feet (2 meters) long. It was made from wood and
bamboo, and reinforced with palm stems called rattan. The shaft was
lacquered to make it waterproof. The bowstring was made from tough
plant fibers, such as hemp or ramie.

The Shortbow

The shortbow, or *hanyu*, was used in battle. It varied between
6 inches (15 cemtimeters) and 6.6 ft (2 m) long. The shortbow became
popular in the Sengoku period, when foot soldiers needed smaller
weapons that were easier to handle.

Arrows

Arrows were often made from reeds and they
varied in size according to their purpose. In battle,
samurai often used steel arrows. These arrows
were strong enough to **concuss** enemies if they hit
the enemies' helmets.

WHAT'S IN A NAME?

Men of the Bow

It is believed that samurai were once
referred to as "men of the bow," because
they often fought with bows and arrows.

The Samurai Sword

The samurai sword was an important weapon because it was believed to represent a samurai's spirit. During the Tokugawa shogunate, swords became a display of rank because only samurai were allowed to carry them. In battle, samurai used three main types of swords.

❖ The *katana* was a long sword that hung from a samurai's belt. The curved blade was around 24 in (60 cm) long, and the sword was used with two hands. Early in the feudal period, the *katana* was straight. Around the 1200s and 1300s it became curved.

❖ The *wakizashi* was a shorter version of the *katana*. The blade was about 12 in (30 cm) long, and the sword was used with one hand.

❖ The *nodachi* was often used by ronin. It could be more than 28 in (70 cm) long, and was usually black. The blade was steel, or a combination of steel and iron. The **scabbard** often had a diamond pattern on the grip.

Samurai often carried several swords at the same time.

The Samurai Pole

Samurai sometimes fought using long poles with blades attached to the ends. The length of the poles allowed samurai to keep their enemies at a distance. In battle, samurai used two main types of poles.

❖ The *naginata* was a long, wooden pole with a curved blade at the point. The pole was about 10 ft (3 m) long and the blade was between 24 in (60 cm) and 6 ft (1.8 m) long. There was usually a sword guard, or a *tsuba*, attached between the blade and the pole. During the Edo period, the *naginata* was seen as a female's weapon.

❖ The *nagamaki* was similar to the *naginata*, but it had a long, thin blade at its tip. It was held with two hands. The **hilt** was covered in sharkskin and wrapped in cord, which allowed samurai to grip it securely. The *nagamaki* was popular between the 1200s and the 1400s.

Daughters of samurai were expected to practice and even fight in battle with the *naginata*.

IN PROFILE: Oda Nobunaga

In Profile

NAME: Oda Nobunaga

ALSO KNOWN AS: Daimyo Nobunaga

BORN: 1534

DIED: 1582

Oda Nobunaga was an important daimyo during the Sengoku period, a time in which clans fought against one another. He overthrew the Ashikaga shogunate and **expelled** its shogun from Kyoto in 1573.

Oda Nobunaga was the first person to attempt to unify Japan. Although he did not achieve this before his death, he did manage to unite a large part of Japan. Nobunaga was also an **innovative** leader who implemented new strategies that helped Japan to increase its power. The unification of Japan was completed by the shoguns of the Tokugawa shogunate after his death.

Notable Moment

In 1560, Nobunaga and his army of 3,000 samurai took Imagawa Yoshimoto's army of 25,000 samurai by surprise at the Battle of Okehazama. Nobunaga's army defeated Yoshimoto's army.

Oda Nobunaga Timeline

1560   1565   1570

1560
Wins the Battle of Okehazama

1561
Forges an alliance between two longstanding warring clans, the Oda clan and the Matsudaira clan

1562
Captures Inabayama Castle

An Innovative Leader

Oda Nobunaga is viewed as an innovative leader because he is believed to have:

❖ used his wealth to support the arts

❖ built iron-clad ships and stone castles that were difficult to destroy

❖ built roads to increase trade and move armies more quickly

❖ appointed people based on ability, not only on rank and family connections

❖ used firearms called *arquebuses* in battle for the first time

What You Should Know About...

Oda Nobunaga

❖ In 1571, Nobunaga attacked Enryakuji Temple and burned it to the ground, killing anyone in his path.

❖ In 1576, Nobunaga ordered the building of Azuchi Castle. It is believed to be Japan's first stone castle.

❖ There are different reports about how Nobunaga died. Some sources claim that there was a **conspiracy** against Nobunaga and that he was murdered by one of his generals. Others claim that he lost a battle at Takamatsu Castle and was forced to commit **seppuku**.

Oda Nobunaga was responsible for the building of Azuchi Castle, which still stands today.

1575

1580

1585

1573
Defeats the Asakura and Azai clans

1576
Orders Japan's first stone castle to be built beside Lake Biwa

1582
Dies during the siege of Takamatsu Castle

Samurai Ranks and Privileges

During the 1400s, the **social status** of the samurai rose until they became one of the highest social classes in feudal Japan. Samurai privileges increased as their status grew.

Samurai Ranks

Different ranks of samurai were given different privileges and it was almost impossible for a samurai to change his rank. By the 1100s, three clear ranks of samurai had been established.

❖ Mounted samurai were high-ranking samurai. They reported directly to the shogun, and fought on horseback.

❖ Foot soldiers were middle-ranking samurai. They fought with swords.

❖ House men, or kenin, were low-ranking samurai. They had administrative duties.

Mounted samurai were wealthy and cultured. Boys born into these families trained to become samurai from a young age. They were also educated in Japan's history, arts, and culture. Ronin and kenin paid taxes and pledged their loyalty to daimyo, who in turn rewarded them with land. They were only allowed to marry women from their own rank.

Mounted samurai had a higher social rank than ronin or kenin.

Privileges

Samurai had many privileges that those in lower social classes did not have. Samurai could carry a long sword and a short sword, whereas peasants, artisans, and merchants were not allowed to carry weapons. Those in lower social classes were expected to show respect to the samurai, and over time samurai were awarded the privilege of **beheading** any peasant who offended them. Samurai could also have their own family crest and surname.

During the feudal period, ronin could carry swords such as this.

Bushido

Bushido is the code of moral principles that Japanese samurai lived by. It was developed between the 800s and the 1100s, and it has roots in four schools of thought or religions:

❖ Buddhism
❖ Confucianism
❖ Zen
❖ Shintoism

Quick Facts

How Did Religion Influence Bushido?
Bushido was based on many values taken from different religions.

❖ Buddhism teaches that people are reborn after death. Samurai learned not to fear death.

❖ Confucianism teaches about relationships with others. Samurai valued relationships, such as those between masters and servants, fathers and sons, and husbands and wives.

❖ Zen teaches meditation and self-belief, and to set no limits. Samurai used these teachings to ward off fear.

❖ Shintoism teaches loyalty. Samurai pledged to be loyal to the emperor, the shogun, and other high-ranking samurai.

The Bushido Code

The Bushido code has seven key virtues:

❖ **rectitude**, or *gi* (義)
❖ courage, or *yū* (勇)
❖ **benevolence**, or *jin* (仁)
❖ respect, or *rei* (礼)
❖ honesty, or *makoto* (誠) or *shin* (信)
❖ honor and glory, or *meiyo* (名誉)
❖ loyalty, or *chūgi* (忠義)

Seppuku was often performed using a tanto sword.

Outside of battle, hara-kiri was performed in a ceremony and samurai wore full ceremonial dress.

Seppuku

The importance of dying an honorable death was at the center of the Bushido code. Seppuku is **ritual suicide** that defeated, wounded, or disgraced samurai could perform to keep their honor intact. It was seen as an act of bravery.

Hara-kiri

The most common form of seppuku was hara-kiri, which means "stomach cutting." To perform this act, samurai sliced open their **abdomen**, which was believed to release their spirit. Hara-kiri was an extremely painful way to die, yet it had to be performed without showing any fear or pain. Sometimes a loyal assistant was allowed to cut the samurai's neck, in order to hasten his death. Hara-kiri was mainly performed on battlefields.

Fortifications and Castles

Samurai relied on fortifications, or defensive structures, to protect their homes and land. Throughout the Heian period, wooden palisades and towers were the main fortifications. During the feudal period, stone walls and castles were built.

Wooden Palisades and Towers

Soldiers during the Heian period built wooden palisades and towers to stop enemy armies from entering their lands. Palisades are wooden walls made from tree trunks, sticks, and branches. Samurai sharpened branches and logs at one end and then set them in a row, with the sharpened ends pointing toward the enemy. Wooden towers were built in order for samurai to see approaching enemies.

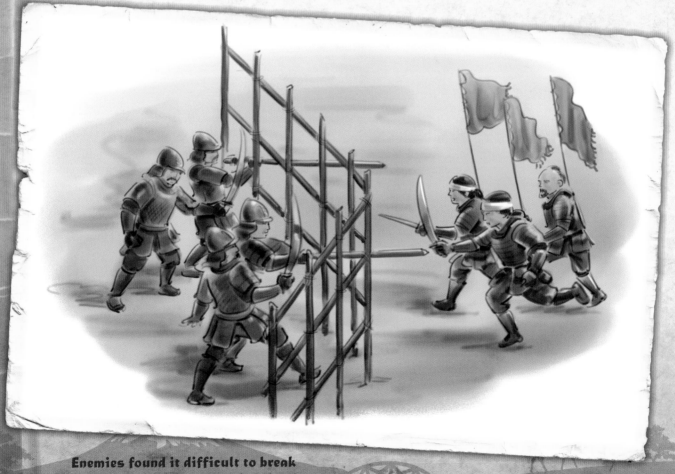

Enemies found it difficult to break through the sharp samurai palisades.

Stone Walls

Stone walls were built to stop armies from landing and to protect castles during battle. The first stone walls were built around the 1100s and, by the 1300s, many daimyo had built stone walls to protect their castles. In 1276, the Kamakura shogunate ordered 15 miles (24 kilometers) of stone wall to be built at Hakata Bay, in order to stop the Mongol army from landing. The wall was around 6.6 ft (2 m) high and about 3.3 ft (1 m) wide at the top, and it still stands today.

Stone Castles

Stone castles were built to protect families from enemies and to demonstrate a family's social status. Many castles were built on mountain tops so that samurai had clear views of approaching enemies. It has been estimated that up to 40,000 castles existed during the Sengoku period. Battles were fought and governments were run from these castles. Today, only about fifty of these castles remain intact.

Matsumoto Castle was built around the 1600s and still stands in its original form today.

IN PROFILE: Shibata Katsuie

In Profile

NAME: Shibata Katsuie

ALSO KNOWN AS: Oni Shibata

BORN: 1530

DIED: 1583

Shibata Katsuie was born into a small branch of the Shiba clan and rose to the role of military commander during the Sengoku period. He served under Oda Nobunaga, an important daimyo of the Sengoku period.

Shibata Katsuie had many victories in battle and he expanded the Shiba clan's **territories**. For his loyalty and success Katsuie was rewarded with Kitanosho Castle.

Notable Moment

In 1573, Katsuie and 400 men were **besieged** by 4,000 enemy soldiers at Chokoji Castle. He launched raids on **enemy lines** and forced them into retreat. Eventually, he won the battle with an all-out attack. This, combined with other victories, led him to become known as *Oni Shibata*. An oni is an ogre in Japanese folklore. The word is often used to indicate someone who is **invincible** or has superhuman strength.

Shibata Katsuie Timeline

1565   1570   1575

1567
Defeats enemy armies in the Settsu province

1573
Given Kitanosho Castle after gaining control of Echizenin

Committing Seppuku

Once Katsuie lost the Battle of Shizugatake, he committed seppuku. Before he died, Katsuie set fire to his castle. He begged his wife to leave with their two daughters. His wife allowed the daughters to leave, but she decided to die with him.

Like many samurai who committed seppuku, Katsuie wrote a death poem before his suicide. The poem is translated as "Fleeting dream paths, in the autumn night! O bird of the mountain, carry my name beyondthe clouds."

What You Should Know About...

Shibata Katsuie

❖ In 1157, Katsuie plotted against Oda Nobunaga. Nobunaga discovered the plot but decided to spare him. As a result, Katsuie pledged undying loyalty to Nobunaga for the rest of his days.

❖ Katsuie committed seppuku at the end of a battle that he did not fight in.

Shibata Katsuie led samurai troops in the Battle of Shizugatake.

Art by Sid Ka'imi Campbell

1580	1585	1590

1581
Begins a **military campaign** at Etchu Province

1582
Suffers an attack that leaves him vulnerable and isolated, as his allies are defeated

1583
Commits seppuku after being defeated at the Battle of Shizugatake

The Decline of the Japanese Samurai

Throughout the feudal period, samurai remained the only armed force in Japan. However, during the Tokugawa shogunate, Japan lived in peace and the samurai were no longer as needed.

The Collapse of Feudal Japan

The end of the Tokugawa shogunate marked the end of feudal Japan. In 1867, the last shogun resigned and the emperor regained power as the head of Japan. Japan's feudal system and the privileges of the samurai class were abolished.

The Decline of the Samurai

The samurai began to fall into decline toward the end of the feudal period. Between 1603 and 1867, the country lived in peace and the samurai had few opportunities for battle. In 1873, the emperor ruled against the samurai, who had sought the right to be Japan's only warriors. An army of paid professional soldiers was established. These soldiers were trained in using guns and they had sophisticated battle tactics. They soon **usurped** the samurai.

The samurai were replaced by a new army of professional soldiers armed with guns.

Glossary

abdomen   The area of the body that holds the stomach, intestines, liver, spleen, and pancreas.

aristocracy   A class that held titles and power that were passed down through families.

armored   Wrapped in a protective covering.

beheading   Cutting off someone's head while they are still alive.

benevolence   Performing good acts or acts of charity.

besieged   Surrounded by enemies.

civil wars   Wars between two groups in their own country.

clans   Groups of Japanese families related by blood or marriage.

components   Parts.

concuss   Cause a temporary brain injury that may lead to confusion, memory loss, or loss of consciousness.

consolidate   Strengthen.

conspiracy   A secret agreement to perform a wrongful act.

conquer   Defeat using force.

daimyo   The highest-ranked members of the samurai nobility, who ran the shogun's lands and estates.

elite   The best or most skilled.

emperor   The ruler of feudal Japan, with similar power to a king.

enduring   Lasting, or used over a long period of time.

enemy lines   The first lines of an enemy's soldiers during a battle.

expelled   Thrown out.

figurehead   A leader with little or no real power.

hierarchy   A series of groupings of people within a social system.

hilt   The handle of a weapon or tool.

imperial family   Those in the emperor's extended family who performed official duties.

inheritance   Passed down through a family.

innovative   Forward-thinking and interested in new ideas.

invincible   Cannot be beaten or conquered.

monarch   A type of government ruler, such as an emperor.

monarchy   A type of government ruled by a single, self-appointed person, such as an emperor.

nobility   A rank given to many wealthy and important people.

provinces   Parts of a country that have been divided up by the government.

recruiting   Enrolling people in military service.

rectitude   Having sound morals or being honorable and honest.

resigned   To have formally given up a political office.

ritual suicide   Killing oneself to maintain honor.

scabbard   A sheath, or case, for a blade or sword.

seppuku   Ritual suicide by taking out the organs, often by performing hara-kiri.

social status   The position of a person in a group of people.

succeeded   Took over, usually from a relative.

territories   Areas of land.

usurped   Took the place of.

Index